UNDERSTANDING MARXISM

"This is an excellent little book and will be a good read for anyone wanting to introduce themselves to Marx's key ideas, particularly around the issues of democracy, or to anyone wanting to refresh their understanding."

—GRAHAM KIRKWOOD, *COUNTERFIRE*

"*Understanding Marxism* is a pro-proletarian primer to help the masses comprehend some of the basics of a complicated worldview, as Wolff identifies some of the capitalist system's essential contradictions."

—ED RAMPELL, JOURNALIST

"For someone new to Marxism, *Understanding Marxism* could be, at first, a flashlight illuminating a pathway through a dark hallway. For someone gaining familiarity with Marxism (possibly the same reader just described, some time later), this book could be a floor plan of the overall layout of the theory's structure."

—ZOE SHERMAN, *DOLLARS & SENSE*

UNDERSTANDING MARXISM

Richard D. Wolff

Haymarket Books
Chicago, Illinois

© Richard Wolff 2018

First published in 2018 by Democracy at Work.

Published in 2025 by
Haymarket Books
P.O. Box 180165
Chicago, IL 60618
www.haymarketbooks.org

ISBN: 979-8-88890-458-9

Distributed to the trade in the US through Consortium
Book Sales and Distribution (www.cbsd.com) and interna-
tionally through Ingram Publisher Services International
(www.ingramcontent.com).

This book was published with the generous support of
Lannan Foundation, Wallace Action Fund, and Marguerite
Casey Foundation.

Special discounts are available for bulk purchases by organizations and institutions. Please email info@haymarket-
books.org for more information.

Cover and book design by Jamie Kerry.

Printed in Canada by union labor.

Library of Congress Cataloging-in-Publication data is
available.

10 9 8 7 6 5 4 3 2 1

CONTENTS

PREFACE

Brexit, Trump, and the global anti-immigrant, anti-foreigner, right-wing wave show just how deeply troubled capitalism is after the 2008 crash. They replicate what happened in many places after capitalism's 1929 crash. Millions are frightened by economic decline. Neither education nor media nor engagement with critical political movements had prepared them for another crash and the subsequent lost decade that lingers. So many strike out in rage and desperation for change that might somehow help reverse the threatening downward spiral.

Given the previous half century of Cold War and its effects on politics, culture and ideology, it was hardly surprising that major early surges of political protest took right-wing forms. Millions turned against political establishments that presided over the economic forces that led to the crash, then bailed out those who caused it and imposed harsh austerities on all those victimized by it. Voting socialist mostly failed as major socialist parties had accommodated to the dominant neoliberalism.

Now some grasp the error they made even as others reproduce it. Those frustrated with the capitalist system search for and find better answers than merely ousting political establishments. Wanting deeper, more critical analyses of what went so badly wrong in contemporary society and political economy, they dare ask . . . about system change.

Thus they find their way to the critique of capitalism stemming from the Marxian tradition, and discover all that it has to offer. All that was kept from political, academic, and mediatic discourses for so long.

There are rising demands for accessible introductions to Marxism and to the social changes it suggests. This essay responds to that interest. It seeks to provide bases for real solutions now that the flaws and failures of contemporary capitalism are exposed: goods delivered chiefly to the 1%, the rest mocked with outrageous inequality, instability, and grossly reactionary political leaders.

Marxism always was the critical shadow of capitalism. Their interactions changed them both. Now Marxism is once again stepping into the light as capitalism shakes from its own excesses and confronts decline. Hopefully this essay can help our era's renewal of Marxism.

INTRODUCTION

T hink of yourself and the people you know who worry about losing jobs and losing incomes. We are struggling, even if we can't always put it into words, with the fact that we're caught up in a relationship where, whatever the work is that we do, there's somebody—the employer—in a position to take the job away. That someone else is in a position to make it impossible for us to pay our bills, keep our home, keep our kids in the schools they know. How did that power get vested in somebody whom we barely know and whose bottom line is profit, not us? Employers live and struggle with this economic system too. They don't trust us, do they? That's why they put cameras in the workplace, hire supervisors to monitor us, and spy on the computers we use. Distrust and all other forms of class conflict and struggle float through our consciousness and shape our lives.

Once we're aware, we can see visible signs of class struggle all the time. There are so many ways that employers constantly try to make more money, more profits, at the employees' expense. We employees, individually and collectively, have to fight it sooner or later. The class struggle that puts employers against employees is always visible at our workplaces or just below the surface there. Then there are also the more invisible ways the class struggle plays out. Those include the disrespect employers show us that we unconsciously take home into our families; the employers' failure to make workplaces safe, healthy, and secure; and their secrecy in making decisions that affect us without our participation or even knowledge.

The class struggle is everywhere; it influences everything and everyone in our society. Marx is the theoretician who first explained it systematically. He opened the way, and those who came after him built on his work. In that way, the class struggle at the core of modern capitalism got attention and analysis. Marxist insights into class struggle have fueled and shaped countless criticisms of capitalism and countless social movements for change beyond it. The criticisms and movements continue today. Yet some still pretend that class struggle isn't there. They say that we need not study the Marxian tradition of thought even though it is the single most developed analysis of class struggles in theory and in history. Theirs is a childish form of ideological blindness that produces ignorance.

Marxism displays a central, crucial focus on the class struggle that both haunts and drives capitalism. It is a tradition that has accumulated theories and historical accounts of class struggles and also provoked reflections on, and debates over, the theories and the histories. Their shared focus constitutes a critique of capitalism that is linked to the pursuit of transition beyond it to a better, more democratic economic system. Nothing could be more relevant and useful here and now to help us understand and cope with the threatening global capitalism of our times. Of course, Marxism's rapid global spread and multiplicity of component theories drew the attention of diverse political actors. How the tradition was understood and used by some Marxists aroused others to disagree. Marxism has always included disagreement and debate—as is true, likewise, of all other global movements of thought and action (e.g., Christianity, Islam, liberalism, democracy, etc.). Abstracting from those disagreements and debates—as in referring to Marxism as some singular theory or practice or policy—usually entails ignorance or distorting simplification. Marxism is not reducible to Stalinism any more than Christianity is reducible to the Catholic Inquisition or than monarchy is reducible to King Charle's regime in today's UK.

Marx himself was a student of philosophy from ancient to modern times. As part of a certain scholarly tradition, he believed that you can best make an original contribution after you have mastered what those before you came to understand. Thus Marx was a close student of Plato and Aristotle as well as the many other great Greek thinkers. He likewise examined the great Catholic thinkers of Medieval times such as Sts.

Augustine and Aquinas. The giants of modern German philosophy, especially Kant and his teacher Hegel, were crucial to Marx's work. Yet he did not, like so many others, limit himself to a narrow pursuit of one discipline. He was an avid student of literature (he loved and often quoted from Shakespeare and Dante and Mozart's operas). He also studied the French revolutionary tradition of what we might now call political science (Danton, Robespierre, Rousseau) and the British tradition of what we now call economics (Smith, Ricardo, and Malthus). In short, Marx's work was a masterful bringing together of many strands of human thought to apply to and understand the capitalist system of Marx's time. A key feature of Marx's approach was explicitly to make his understanding serve the goal of social transformation.

Marx's approach proved extraordinarily powerful and effective. His writings persuaded people around the world, such that Marxism became an important tradition of thought and movement for social change across the globe. It remains so. It has been an indispensable resource for all kinds of transformative movements but especially for those that included a demand and desire to break out of and beyond the capitalist economic system. To an immense diversity of social movements beyond slavery, feudalism, imperialism, etc., Marx contributed an understanding of their interdependence with class struggles to move beyond capitalism. Marxism thus always carried visions of a socialism beyond capitalism.

The visions ranged from utopias to practical proposals to actually existing experiments in constructing socialist alternatives. Marxists always debated and contested both their multiple, different interpretations of the tradition and their multiple and different assessments of how the various socialisms challenged capitalism. Equating Marxism in the singular with socialism in the singular exposes an ignorance of the diversity and richness of both traditions.

For us in the US to recognize Marxism as a rich tradition from which we can learn much, we must clear away much Cold War debris. For the last 75 years, a sustained effort sought to demonize Marxism. That effort's leaders, the "business community" and most of those it enriched, saw the New Deal and the World War II alliance with the Soviet Union as an existential threat. Those leaders' power, prestige, and wealth were challenged by a frightening social upsurge from below. Socialism was their enemies' goal, and Marxism was their theory and strategy driving toward socialism. Just as the US moved globally to unseat and end the old colonialism of the Europeans, it also established a new, informal neocolonialism run by and for the US. In pure projection, the US-initiated, post-1945 Cold War hyped a "Soviet threat to rule the world." In fact, the USSR was a minor obstacle to the US's global neocolonialism. That the USSR was much poorer, still industrially backward in many ways, and barely able to defend itself against a much smaller Germany was swept aside. Instead, postwar US capitalism has driven relentlessly to reverse its reforms from below since 1929 and erase memories of its cyclically bedeviled system's worst crash ever.

The US's Cold War opposition to Marxism also entailed a caricature that rendered Marxism as a particularly unwelcome version of extreme Keynesianism. In this caricature, Marxism is the theoretical rationale for a dictatorship of the state as against "private enterprises and free markets." In this caricature, business and personal freedom and liberty are all forcibly suppressed in deference to socialist central planners' preferences and plans. Marxism could thus be demonized as the enemy of private property, private enterprise, the market, freedom, and liberty. Keynesianism—as New Deal economic policy came to be known—could then likewise be associated with Marxism to further its demonization as well.

This caricaturization of Marxism becomes a rather thin propaganda tool for state economic controls and ultimately for state dictatorship. It functions as a statist straw man that social democrats, liberals, neoliberals, and libertarians have long specialized in denouncing. But it is often true of politically effective caricatures that they contain grains of truth. Among twentith-century Marxists, there were some whose interpretations came close to the critics' caricatures. However, there were also always Marxists with very different, clashing interpretations. Debates among Marxists over clashing interpretations were intense and ongoing throughout the last 150 years. Especially over the last 30 years since the USSR's implosion, those debates have increasingly challenged, opposed, and offered alternative interpretations to those close to the hostile caricature. To ignore the debates characterizing Marxism is not only historically and theoretically unjustified; it is also a dishonest part of the demonizing caricature.

The Cold War suppression of Marxism in the US took many forms. Jobs and incomes were lost, forcing the afflicted into careers far removed from their educations and passions. Teachers, civil servants of all kinds, artists (writers, musicians, actors, etc.), union officials, and many others were deprived of positions of respect and influence in their communities. Some were arrested, imprisoned, or deported. A carefully cultivated atmosphere emerged that taught millions to avoid and suspect even the most moderate of leftist speech, writing, etc. The Cold War deprived US residents of opportunities to learn from the Marxian tradition, including its debates and changes. Marxism's already great influence around the world by 1945 should have been enough to justify keeping abreast of that tradition's evolution. But so intense were campaigns to reverse the New Deal and extinguish the "red menace," that suppression utterly blocked engagement. Criticism of capitalism became disloyalty; advocacy of a change toward socialism became treason.

Hysterical defensiveness shut down open, honest debate over the strengths and weaknesses of capitalism versus socialism. Everything was reduced to an extreme, crude we-versus-them mentality.

My personal trajectory can illustrate some of these Cold War effects. Born in Ohio, I am a product of US schooling, including its "elite" universities: undergraduate at Harvard, master's in economics from Stanford, and PhD in economics from Yale. I spent 10 years of my life in those three institutions, two semesters per year. During those 20 semesters, concentrated mostly on history and economics, we studied the capitalist economic system 99 percent of the time. For 19 of those 20 semesters, our assignments included not one word of Marx nor of Marxist critics of capitalism. In one of the 20 semesters, Professor Paul A. Baran taught a course at Stanford that used Marx's theories that we were assigned to read and discuss. As an isolated, exceptional academic, Baran confirmed explicitly what I had come to understand implicitly. So total (totalitarian) was the demonization of Marxism that even the intellectuals, in and out of academia, were afraid to go anywhere near it, to look at it, to read it, to think about it, to risk being thought of as "interested in" Marxism.

When I completed my doctoral dissertation at Yale University and was preparing to defend it in the usual official formality, I informed my dissertation committee (senior faculty) that I wanted to title my dissertation

"The Economics of Colonialism: Britain in Kenya." I was told that that title was unacceptable and would prevent my being granted the PhD. When I asked why, I was told that "colonialism" was a "value-laden" term not suitable for objective, scientific analysis. My dissertation's title was thus changed to "Economic Aspects of British Foreign Policy: Britain and Kenya." It did not matter that I had studied files on Kenya in London at the British Colonial [sic] Office Library, spent time in Kenya, learned Swahili, and otherwise performed all the requirements for the PhD. So intense was the hysteria—many Marxist critiques of capitalist imperialism had been provoked by the US war in Vietnam—that the very word had to be expunged. The atmosphere was toxic, the official Yale response childish. I got the PhD.

In choosing which of many such vignettes to relate here I cannot use some even now. I still need to protect individuals who use Marxism in their work—that is often widely praised and approved—by not mentioning their names in association with that use. So let me conclude these personal reflections with a story about my years as a Harvard undergraduate. I majored in history there and graduated magna cum laude (lots of As). I had met a Marxist scholar who lived in Cambridge, Fritz Pappenheim. He kindly spent many hours discussing and effectively tutoring me in Marxism, which I appreciated enormously. Nothing remotely similar was available at Harvard. When my courses at Harvard assigned term papers for students to prepare, I would discuss them with Fritz and ask his help in using the assignment to include research into what Marxists had written about specific topics I chose. He gave me bibliographies and answered questions that arose as I read through them. The papers I wrote and handed in often got not merely an A grade but comments about the "originality" of my approach, the "interesting connections" drawn between economic history and other histories, and so on. Fritz and I laughed often since we both knew that what I composed in my papers was a first, relatively crude and somewhat mechanical application of Marxism. I got As because my professors knew little or nothing about Marxism or its literature on the topics they assigned to us. In effect, they gave Marx the A by giving it to my paper. They just did not know they were doing so. Their studied ignorance of Marx was that total.

Generations of students at all levels of public and private education in the US have thus been systematically excluded from anything reasonably like "learning about Marxism." They are unable to use Marxist methods of analysis alongside others to address and solve analytical and practical problems. They have been hampered in identifying and overcoming weaknesses and absences in non-Marxist theories and analyses because they did not encounter or take seriously the Marxist criticisms of those non-Marxist theories and analyses. For example, where Marxist theories have informed policy in relationship to the business cycles afflicting capitalism, economies have suffered less from those cycles because preparations for such cycles and policies to contain them were more successful. Both the USSR and China illustrate that point. Had Marxist-informed critiques of capitalism's tendency towards ever-greater inequalities of wealth and income distributions been studied systematically, that tendency could have been given the attention it deserves. Indeed, as the critics of capitalism increase in number and their critiques become all the more influential, ever more Americans believe and feel that capitalism is a declining system. They therefore seek alternatives to consider. Marxism has both theories and concrete empirical examples to offer to such seekers, but the suppression of the Marxian tradition still blocks many Americans' awareness of, let alone familiarity with, its insights about post-capitalist economic systems.

Marx's insights about the class differences in society and about the capitalist class struggles that shape our society are useful and powerful. Are they all 100 percent right? Of course not. Do we have to develop, change, and adjust them to our circumstances? Yes, of course. Marx intended neither a religion nor a dogma. Some Marxists later made it that. Human history includes many examples of sets of profound, open ideas transformed into religions or dogmas. To engage Marxian theories does not require treating them as a religion or a dogma. But to refuse to learn about and use them to understand society and social change—that is self-destructive. Such willful blindness contradicts real education. It reflects a society so fearful about its basic system that it cannot allow discussion and debate among its critics—even when many Marxists among them have been responsible enough to offer ways out of and from capitalism to alternative, better social systems.

The capitalist system is now grappling with fundamental contradictions. Its old centers (Western Europe, North America, and Japan) are now fading as new centers of dynamic growth take hold in China, India, Brazil, and so forth. Capitalist globalization confronts a major, historic backlash that it may not survive. Business cycles underscore capitalism's instability. Capitalism's generation of unequal income and wealth distributions is "off the chart." Capitalism's use and abuse of nature and technology are questioned, challenged, and opposed as never before.

The COVID-19 catastrophe can illustrate the useful insights made possible by the Marxian tradition's critical perspective. Consider that the US had a similar pandemic experience a century earlier with what then was called the "Spanish flu." Likewise US authorities knew about more recent, well-known dangerous flu epidemics (SARS, MERS, Ebola, etc.). What the US needed (and could well afford) was a plentiful supply of tests, masks, ventilators, and hospital ICUs to be prepared for the next virus. Moreover, these supplies needed to be strategically stored in protected, monitored, and secure warehouses and medical buildings near population centers. The US has the physical and organizational capabilities to meet all these needs. However, it did not do so. Private US capitalist enterprises could have but did not produce the supplies to meet the needs.

Those private enterprises acted in accordance with the logic of capitalism: They maximized profits by choosing not to produce and store the needed supplies. They made that decision because the costs of producing and warehousing the supplies for unknown periods of time before the next virus or other disease threatened was more risky and less profitable than alternative investment possibilities that they in fact chose. The key problem was the system. Capitalist employers, a minority, made a profit-driven decision that afflicted a majority, the mass of employees systemically excluded from making that decision. Had the relevant enterprises operated as democratic worker cooperatives (where majority rule governed decisions by all participants, each with an equal vote in reaching that decision), all those affected by a life-and-death decision would have had an equal say in making it. In evaluating the profit versus the health implications of the decision, the mass of employees were prevented by capitalism from playing any role. The alternative worker co-op organization of enterprises would have enabled workers to participate in making that decision. That would then have been a democratic decision and might well have resulted in an altogether different preparation for and experience of COVID-19 for the US.

Another example develops the Marxist criticism further. The Biden regime faced two huge economic problems:

(1) how to fund a major updating of a crumbling infrastructure

(2) how to reduce the extreme inequality of wealth in the US.

Marxist criticisms have shown the irrationality and inefficiency—for US capitalism as a whole—of both dilapidated infrastructure and extremely unequal wealth. The appropriate policy that would quite likely have flowed from replacing hierarchical capitalist enterprise organization with a democratic workers cooperative organization would have targeted both problems with the same solution. A graduated wealth tax could have done that. Biden's regime had not proposed, let alone implemented, such a policy. Marxists could have and would have made such policies part of the national discussion about national economic policy.

If you want to understand capitalism, if you want to make society better, then Marx's contribution is to draw your attention to capitalist production's core class conflict. That conflict's multiple, profound social consequences are what Marx's *Capital* and other works explain and explore. Especially if you want to make society better, it is self-defeating to pretend that class struggle is not there. Such a pretense is like pretending that there is no difference between how we in the US treat males and females, rich and poor people, whites and people of color, etc. Most Americans know that these are important differences that entail problems we must address and overcome if the US is ever to realize its social potential. Marx explains that solving capitalism's problems requires similarly acknowledging and overcoming its class structure, conflict, and struggles. No one has studied those conflicts more than Marx and the tradition he initiated.

Marxism is worth understanding. It offers new directions for social development beyond and better than the capitalism we have. That is why Democracy at Work wrote and published this book, and why we have produced this new introduction for the hardcover edition. The positive reactions of readers have mounted far beyond our expectations. The demonstrated appetite to understand the Marxist tradition of thought and action prompted us to produce an eBook and now this hardcover edition. Our goal was, and remains, to explain and share our excitement about the ways in which Marxism helps us to critically rethink capitalism today.

This book is an introduction. Its greatest success would be if it piqued your interest to learn and use more of Marxism.

UNDERSTANDING
MARXISM

66 The history of all hitherto existing society is the history of class struggles. 99

CHAPTER 1

Why Understanding Capitalism Today Requires Marxism

We offer this essay now because of the power and usefulness *today* of Marx's criticism of the capitalist economic system. Capitalism has spread since Marx's time to become today's global system. Along the way, it changed in many ways. Yet its core remained a particular kind of economic system, uniquely different from the slave, feudal, and other systems of human history. Capitalism's way of producing and distributing goods and services retains the basic structure, dynamic, flaws, and injustices that Marx so acutely criticized.

Why should we pay attention to the great social critics like Marx? Critics see and understand any society differently from its admirers. To understand anything, intelligent people consider society directly but also consider how others see and understand it. Thus, they

1

consider (1) what those people believe who like it, but also (2) what those people believe who don't like it.

From all those considerations, thoughtful conclusions are drawn.

As an example, imagine wanting to understand the family that lives up the road (mama, papa, and their two kids). Let's suppose we know one kid thinks it's the greatest family there ever was, and the other one thinks it's a basket case of psychological dysfunction. To study the family, it would be bizarre to choose to talk to only one child. Basic honesty would require us to talk with both children, ask questions, hear what each has to say, as well as interview and observe the parents and the family together, etc. On the basis of all that we then draw our own conclusions about that family, making the best judgment we can.

So it is with understanding capitalism. It requires that we consider the system directly but also consider the assessments of critics as well as admirers or celebrants.

This process becomes extra difficult when the larger social context is an extremely polarized confrontation between critics and celebrants of capitalism.

We must all acknowledge that words like "Marx" and "Marxism," "socialism," "communism," and all that, have been scare words for many people for many years. In the US, even before the Cold War erupted, capitalism's defenders and admirers often demonized capitalism's critics as dangerous, disloyal, foreign, and/or anti-American, anti-Christian, and so on. Since 1945, Americans were widely taught, encouraged or pressed to view socialism, communism, Marxism, the USSR, etc. with fear, anxiety, and hatred. Therefore, most Americans paid little or no attention to the work of Karl Marx.

Teachers at all levels either ignored that work or subjected it to brief dismissive treatments. Business leaders, journalists, and academics learned (or rather, did not learn) from those teachers and so replicated their ignorance or dismissals of Marx and Marxism. It took the latest crash of capitalism in 2008 to shock many into the realization that capitalism had remained the same old unstable economic system it had always been. Likewise, American capitalism's rush into extreme inequality undermined the widespread assertion that "capitalism delivers the goods," or at least exposed that it delivered a lot more to the 1% than to the other 99%. The last few years have thus seen a global renewal of critical attitudes toward capitalism. Those evolved quickly into renewed interest in studying what capitalism's critics have to say and offer as a systemic alternative. This essay reflects and also seeks to contribute to those renewals.

For the last 200 years, capitalism's leading critics have been Karl Marx and the diverse tendencies deeply influenced by Marx's work. In other words, Marxism has been the leading tradition of thought and practice critical of capitalism. It represents the ideas and experiences accumulated across generations around the globe who tried and try to move society beyond capitalism using Marx's critical insights. Marx and Marxism are as important on the side of criticizing capitalism as Adam Smith, David Ricardo, and John Maynard Keynes are on the side of those who celebrate capitalism.

" The mode of production of material life determines the social, political and intellectual life process in general. "

CHAPTER 2

Capitalism vs. Slavery and Feudalism

Achievements and Failures

What motivated Karl Marx, as a young man growing up in the middle of nineteenth-century Europe, to become a critic of capitalism? The answer is partly the American and French revolutions of the late eighteenth century. Marx particularly embraced their key demands: in France, liberty, equality, brotherhood and in the US, democracy. He wanted those demands to be realized in modern society. He believed that the capitalism advocated by the French and American revolutionaries was a better system than the feudal, slave, and other previous systems of human history. He believed as well—like so many other young people of his time—that capitalism would bring with it the liberty, equality, brotherhood, and democracy that the French and American revolutionaries had promised it would.

But the roughly 75 years that separated his arrival at adulthood from the French and American revolutions presented Marx with a profoundly challenging contradiction. The revolutions had succeeded in establishing capitalism. It was pulsating and growing all around him in Western Europe. Gone or going were the old economic systems of masters and slaves, lords and serfs. In their places were relatively "free" men and women in the new capitalist system of employers and employees. But the capitalism Marx saw and lived in had not established liberty, equality, fraternity, or real democracy. Moreover, it showed few signs of moving in such directions.

Instead, when Karl Marx looked around the Europe of his time, he saw pretty much what emerged, for example, in the novels of Charles Dickens (or of Émile Zola, Maxim Gorky, and Jack London). He found an enormous gap between a relatively small part of the population that was well off, well educated, literate, and comfortable, and a mass of agricultural, industrial and service workers who were suffering: poor, uneducated, and often illiterate. Marx felt that capitalism had betrayed the promise that had led so many people he admired to support ending feudalism, slavery, etc., with bloody revolutions where needed. Capitalism had failed to deliver liberty, equality, fraternity, and democracy.

And so he set himself a goal. "What happened?" was the great question for him. Why did capitalism not keep its promise? Had it tried and failed? And if so, why? The research he undertook, which he and his closest associates then wrote up, comprises Marx's contribution, his critical understanding of capitalism.

He discovered that the reason why capitalism failed to realize liberty, equality, fraternity, and democracy, was that its own structure and social effects were themselves obstacles to realizing those lofty goals. In making that discovery, Marx retained those goals as his own.

Marx eventually drew the conclusion that genuine progress toward achieving liberty, equality, fraternity, and democracy required a change of economic system from capitalism to what he called socialism.

The research that led to this conclusion was deeply historical. The history of economic systems before capitalism provided Marx with crucial clues. The two systems on which Marx focused his attention were slavery and feudalism.

Slave economic systems divide the human beings engaged in producing and distributing goods and services into two groups: masters and slaves. Wealth, power and cultural dominance lie exclusively in the hands of the masters. Slaves are the property of masters. In general, slaves do the work of production and distribution while masters mostly supervise the slaves. Past slave societies were shaped, governed and run by the masters, who reproduced the system across time. Masters wanted to stay masters; their children became masters in turn. If you were born into that society as a slave, you almost always remained a slave, and your children would be slaves. In their relationship to masters, slaves partook very little of liberty, equality, fraternity, or democracy.

In feudal economic systems, the positions of master and slave disappear and are replaced by lord and serf. In European feudalism, lords supervised and dominated the serfs who did the work, much as the masters had done in relation to slaves. However, while serfs were not property as slaves were, they were born into the social position occupied by their parents, as was the case with slaves.

In relation to slavery and feudalism as economic systems, capitalism was at once different and similar. It was different because the revolutionaries who overthrew previous systems to establish capitalism generally insisted on freeing slaves and serfs from their subordinate position and declaring all free and equal. None could be bound into slave-like or serf-like servitudes; thus they could enjoy liberty from those servitudes.

Finally, capitalism's defenders and advocates generally supported political democratization extending the one-person-one-vote in politics to ever-larger proportions of adult populations.

Capitalism was, however, similar to slavery and feudalism in a central, crucial dimension. Marx establishes this central point early in volume 1 of *Capital* as part of his explanation of "exploitation." In slavery, the slaves produce the goods and services that become entirely—100%—the immediate property of the master (as is the slave). The master decides whether, when, how, and how much of the slaves' output will be returned to the slave for the latter's reproduction (food, clothing, shelter, etc.). This result can be expressed by dividing the length of the slaves' working days into two portions: one is the portion whose products are returned to the slaves for their consumption. Marx called this the slaves' "necessary labor." The second portion of the slaves' labor yields products kept and used by the master; Marx called this "surplus labor." It was labor done by slaves beyond that necessary for whatever level of reproduction masters allowed them.

The same sort of reasoning applies to feudalism. There the serf is assigned land to cultivate part of the time and with the proviso that the products of that time on that land are to be kept by the serf for the consumption of his/her family unit. Another portion of the serf's working time is assigned to be done on the domain of the lord who also keeps the product of that portion. Necessary labor is then what the serf does on the land assigned to him/her, while surplus labor is that portion of the serf's total labor time deployed on the lord's domain. Marx referred to slaves and serfs as "exploited" laborers precisely because (and to the extent that) a portion of their labor and its products were appropriated by persons other than the laborers themselves.

Marx's argument then hits home: capitalism remains like slavery and feudalism because

(1) it too divides the participants producing and distributing goods and services into two groups (employers and employees), and

(2) it too divides the laborer's working day into necessary and surplus portions.

It is merely the forms of these divisions that differ among slavery, feudalism and capitalism; the divisions themselves are substantially the same. In capitalism, the employee agrees to work, say for a week, and to receive their pay Friday afternoon. During the week, the employee's labor contributes to the total product sold by the employer at week's end. The revenue from that total product sold is composed of one part that equals the cost of the inputs used up in producing that total product; that part is normally used to replace those used-up inputs. The rest of the employer's revenue is divided into two portions: one is given to the employee as wages, while the other is retained by the employer for their consumption or use. Wages are the products of the laborer's necessary labor time; revenues retained by the employer are the products of the laborer's surplus labor time. The "free" laborer of capitalism—the person who sells his/

her labor power in exchange for wages—is exploited just like the "unfree" labor of slaves and serfs.

Capitalism, Marx said, never went beyond those economic models where a few dominate a majority. Capitalism just replaced the dichotomies of master/slave and lord/serf with a new one. A dominating and exploiting minority was still there, but it had a new name: employers.

A dominated and exploited majority was still there but with its new name: employees. As had happened with slavery and feudalism, capitalism's dominant minority played and plays the dominant social role. Employers control the politicians and the direction of social development; they make all key decisions in the workplace; they run the show. The masses of people are subordinated.

Marx showed that one key foundation for capitalism's failure to realize liberty, equality, fraternity and democracy was the internal organization of the capitalist enterprise. There, a tiny group of people at the top (major owners and top executives) make all the key decisions regarding what, how, and where to produce and what to do with the fruits of their employees' surplus labor. The employees are systematically excluded from making those decisions, but they must live with the results of those decisions.

That's not democracy; that is its opposite.

Marx died in 1883. In the 135 years since then, his ideas spread to every country on earth. People in very different economic, political, and cultural conditions found enormous meaning in what Marx, and later Marxists, wrote, said, and did. Every country on the planet includes Marxist organizations, Marxist unions, Marxist newspapers, Marxist societies, Marxist political parties and so on. They all found meaning in Marxism, and they still do.

" The human being is in the most literal sense a political animal, not merely a gregarious animal, but an animal which can individuate itself only in the midst of society. "

CHAPTER 3

Employer/Employee

The Core Relationship of Capitalism

A major part of Marx's contribution was in economics. He was a broadly engaged and educated European intellectual of his time when relatively few people were educated or even literate. Formally trained in philosophy, he began his adult working life as a professor of philosophy. However, his interests in the world around him moved him quickly to become what we would nowadays call an economist. Here we present the core finding of his economic studies before following his fascinating elaboration of that core. In every human society, from the earliest records we know to the present, people produce and distribute something Marx called a surplus. We may begin by explaining what Marx meant by this.

In every society, he says, human beings survive by labor: transforming nature to meet their needs. They convert wool into clothing to keep warm, trees to build shelters from the rain and the storm, land into food, and so on. In laboring, humans use their brains and muscles to transform nature into useful consumable products upon which human societies depend.

But *not all* people work, not all use their brains and muscles to transform nature. There are always parts of each human society—large and small—that do not work. Those parts survive if and only if the members of the society who do work *produce more than they themselves consume.* That output exceeding what the workers themselves consume is what Marx means by a surplus. That surplus, if distributed to people other than the workers who produced it, enables such other people to survive and function in the society. Babies are one example of those other people who couldn't possibly use their brains and muscles to transform nature because they haven't managed to stand up yet. Some members of society must produce surpluses if babies are to survive by living off that surplus.

In most societies the producers of surpluses—Marx calls them *productive* laborers precisely *because* they produce a surplus—distribute them to more than the society's babies. Children, the sick, and the elderly are often recipients of surpluses. So too are people capable of producing surpluses, but who do not do so. The surpluses produced by some members of human societies sustain the members who live off the surplus distributed to them. We may begin with an illustrative example of a slave society. When the slave works on a slave plantation, everything he or she produces belongs immediately and automatically to the master. Typically, the master gives a portion of the slave's surplus back to the slave (in the forms of food, clothing, shelter, and so on). The goal is to enable the slave to work again tomorrow. The master uses another portion of the slave's output to replenish the tools, equipment, and raw materials used up during the slave's work.

The rest of what the slave produces is the slave's surplus. Like every other portion of the slave's output, the slave's surplus also belongs to the master. The master takes that surplus and uses it to fund the master's consumption, the master's personal servants and retainers, and any other people whose social activity the master deems necessary to support. The master uses a portion of the slave surplus to support that activity because it helps to reproduce the slave system over which the master presides. For example, the master might pay (distribute a share of the slave surplus to) a group of bandits to capture and return runaway slaves.

The people who live off shares of slave surpluses distributed to them by masters may be engaged in labor using their brains and muscles. But they do not themselves produce surpluses. For that reason, they are, for Marx, *unproductive* laborers. Ever the social critic and theorist, Marx wants to underscore the difference between those workers who produce surpluses from those who live off distributions of surplus from others.

He sees that difference as having all sorts of important implications for the two groups of workers' different attitudes toward the existing system, toward projects of going beyond that system, etc. He likewise underscores the differences between productive and unproductive workers so that what they have in common—for example, they might all be slaves—does not obscure their differences: a matter of the utmost importance for any political project of unifying all slaves into a powerful social force.

The master lives off the surplus. The master does not tend the cotton fields, nor raise the fruits and vegetables, the cheese, the butter, or the meat. The productive slaves do all of that. They produce more cotton than they need to clothe themselves, more food and clothing than they need for themselves, and all that "more"—in kind or else in money if it is marketed—is delivered to the master. The master uses it to keep this kind of society going. The master sits at the top; the master has the power; the master is sustained by the surplus of the slaves.

Much the same logic figures in Marx's analysis of feudalism. The productive workers there are serfs, and the surplus they produce is delivered to the lord. In Europe, the name given to the feudal surplus was "rent." Lords lived off the rents they obtained from the serfs they exploited; they often used those rents to sustain servants, etc., who thus also lived off the feudal surplus as feudalism's unproductive laborers.

Now to Marx's main point: in capitalism, we find the same basic exploitation found inside slave and feudal economic systems. It is disguised in and by the formalities of the employer-employee system. In *Capital*'s first volume, Marx penetrates the disguise to show how the relationship between employer and employee includes the particularly capitalist form of producing and distributing a surplus.

Imagine yourself as a job seeker discussing employment with an employer whose enterprise makes ladders. After going over other details of the job, you come to the wage issue and agree on $20 per hour for a 9 to 5 job from Monday through Friday. The employer believes that employing you—as with all other productive laborers hired—will add quality and/or quantity to the enterprise's output of ladders and thus more sales revenue as well.

Marx then explains what most workers at least instinctively intuit. An employer will only pay a productive worker $20 per hour if during that hour more than $20 worth of sales revenue results. In that more, Marx tells us, lies the surplus in its capitalist form.

The *value added* (to the value of the tools, equipment, and raw materials used up in production) by each worker's hour of labor *exceeds the value paid* to the worker for that hour's labor. The difference between value added and wage paid is the surplus produced by the worker in a capitalist enterprise. The employer captures the surplus within the revenue obtained when the enterprise's output is sold. The employer divides that revenue into three portions. One is used to replace/replenish the tools, equipment, and raw materials used up in producing the enterprise's output. Another portion goes to the hired workers as wages. And the third comprises the surplus retained and thus appropriated by the employing capitalist.

Like the productive labor of slaves and serfs, that of employees is exploited: they all produce surpluses for others. Only the forms of the capitalist surplus and of the capitalist exploitative relationship distinguish them from their parallels in slavery and feudalism.

At the productive core of capitalism, in the relationship there between employer and employee, the latter produces surpluses appropriated by the former. In this exploitation, Marx locates a key obstacle that prevents capitalism from achieving its promised effects of liberty, equality, brotherhood, and democracy. The latter's absences in slavery and feudalism derived likewise from the exploitative relationships at their productive cores. Marx's conclusion follows: to achieve liberty, equality, brotherhood, and democracy in any society, any exploitative production relationship must be excluded.

For a minority to appropriate and distribute the surplus produced by a majority is inconsistent with and undermines the progressive social goals advocated by the French and American revolutions and given lip service everywhere ever since.

Marxist writings have often spoken of "wage slaves." That was not just a casual remark. It links the condition of the wage earner to that of the slave. Looking at wage earners' freedom through the lens of Marx's surplus theory exposes that freedom as illusory. In capitalism, most workers are trapped into being either a wage-earner producing surplus for an employer or else a wage-earner serving an employer and living off the distribution of some other productive worker's surplus. Freedom requires changing the system because otherwise you are forever trapped in it.

Marx argues that exploitative societies typically use their surpluses to maintain that exploitation. Masters use the surplus taken from slaves to maintain slavery; lords use their serfs' surplus to maintain feudalism. Capitalists likewise use the surplus appropriated from productive workers to reproduce the social relations of capitalism, the society of employers and employees. This means giving capitalists—and their delegated representatives—the dominant positions not only in the economy but also in politics and culture.

In capitalism—a hundred years ago, fifty years ago, or right now—it's the employer class that is socially dominant. Marx's contribution was to locate in production the fundamental mechanism whereby this domination is secured.

In his discussion of surpluses and exploitation, Marx developed his own unique concept of class, a concept different from the traditional, pre-Marxist conceptions. Before Marx (indeed, for thousands of years) many people had classified populations into subgroups according to how much wealth they owned or how much power over others they wielded. Those who focused on wealth separated the propertied from the propertyless, the rich from the poor, and, of course, middle classes from those above and below them. Those who focused on power distinguished rulers from ruled, powerful from powerless, etc. For all these people class was a category dividing and thereby describing people according to the distributions of property or power among them. Marx made use of those old concepts (categories, definitions) of class in crafting his social criticism. In this, he followed many who had done likewise before him and were doing the same alongside him.

However, unlike those others, Marx also invented and used another, different concept of class: one based on his surplus analysis. There was the class of surplus producers, the class of surplus appropriators, and the class of those receiving shares of the surplus distributed to them by the appropriators. The conflicts among them undermined capitalists' often-repeated commitments to liberty, equality, brotherhood, and democracy. Put in other terms, Marx invented and used his surplus-based concepts of class to explain why previous social critics of grossly unequal distributions of wealth and power had so far been unable to overcome those social injustices.

They had not understood that changing the organization of the surplus was a necessary accompaniment of any other program aimed to reduce inequalities in the social distributions of wealth and power. They had not understood why ending exploitation was necessary to actualize social commitments to liberty, equality, brotherhood, and democracy. The class conflicts Marx focused his attention on (for example in Marx's three volumes of *Capital*) were chiefly about the production and distribution of the surplus and only secondarily about the social distributions of property and power.

" As in private life one differentiates between what a man thinks and says of himself and what he really is and does, so in historical struggles one must still more distinguish the language and the imaginary aspirations of parties from their real organism and their real interests, their conception of themselves from their reality. "

CHAPTER 4

Employers/ Employees

Capitalism's Struggling Classes

I n modern capitalism, the products of capitalist enterprises take the form of commodities. That means they pass from producer to consumer by means of an intermediate process, namely market exchanges. Capitalist enterprises "buy" their commodity inputs, hire (another word for buy) the labor power of their laborers, and sell the commodity outputs produced by combining inputs and laborers in work.

A distinguishing sign of capitalism is that the ability to work—labor power—itself becomes a commodity to be bought and sold. Labor power was not a commodity in the slave and feudal economic systems.

Capitalist businesses obtain revenues, money earned by selling their output commodities. Their revenues typically exceed the sum of money spent buying input commodities (the tools, equipment, and raw materials used up in production) plus money spent buying labor power. In short, revenues exceed costs of production. That excess is the surplus.

One implication of Marx's analysis is that the class of employers will always seek to reduce the wages paid to their hired, productive laborers. Likewise, employers will always seek to lengthen the time and pace of work.

The reasons for both pressures lie in the simple arithmetic of capitalist exploitation: the greater the value added by the laborers and the smaller the portion returned to them as wages, the greater the surplus acquired by the capitalist.

As we discuss further below, the more surplus the capitalist can get from the surplus-producing laborers, the more funds the capitalist has to consume, grow, compete, and secure the system that puts the capitalist on top.

Productive laborers will likewise always seek higher wages as their standard of living (and that of their family) usually depends on those wages. Class struggle is the unavoidable result of capitalism.

Over the last three centuries, capitalism has successfully reproduced itself while spreading to become the dominant organization of production in the world.

However, as Marx pointed out, capitalism's operations and reproduction were as "efficient" in producing wealth as in producing poverty. Poverty has proved to be a continuing "problem" for capitalism that it never eradicated.

For Marx, to eradicate poverty you need to change to an economic system other than capitalism.

" As capitalist, he is only capital personified. His soul is the soul of capital. But capital has one single life impulse, the tendency to create value and surplus-value, to make its constant factor, the means of production, absorb the greatest possible amount of surplus-labour. "

CHAPTER 5

Producing and Distributing the Surplus in the Capitalist System

We turn next to the *distribution* of capitalist surpluses. That distribution illustrates how capitalism's organization of the surplus deeply influences so many other aspects of societies where it exists (and especially where it prevails). Capitalists distribute significant portions of the surplus they appropriate to themselves for their consumption. They do so both for personal satisfaction and to underscore their differences (in homes, dress, transport, etc.) from the wage earners. The differences in consumption level—*results* of the inequality produced and sustained by capitalism—can then be transformed ideologically into signs of inherent attributes of individuals that make some surplus appropriators and others surplus producers. Just as earlier societies had made the inequalities resulting from slavery and feudalism matters caused rather by nature or God, in capitalism strong ideological tendencies make inherent individual variability ("human nature") the cause. It too, like nature and God, cannot be changed by mere mortals. The passing social convention—made and changed by society—becomes instead moored and unmovable in cement. Those who rule societies need desperately to believe and have others believe their positions are permanent.

Just as importantly, capitalists distribute other portions of the surplus they appropriate to all sorts of managers and supervisors to perform tasks needed for the surplus to be produced. Those tasks are not themselves productive of surpluses, but they are crucial to the production of surplus by others. This distinction matters. The personnel manager in a modern capitalist corporation does not labor with machines to transform raw materials into commodities for sale. Such a manager controls and maneuvers productive laborers but is not one of them. The salary and equipment such a manager uses represent costs to the capitalist defrayed by distributions of the surplus. In capitalism, as Marx makes so clear, the capitalist has to distribute much of the surplus to others in order to keep on getting surplus. Without personnel managers, the surplus-producing workers might produce less surplus or none at all.

The manager in this case is an unproductive laborer. His work provides a necessary condition of existence for surplus production by other, productive laborers. The latter are *performers* of surplus labor; the manager is an *enabler* of their productive labor. For capitalism to reproduce itself, it requires performers *and* enablers, productive *and* unproductive laborers, but that does not mean their differences do not matter. Quite the contrary: in every exploitative economic system, the two different kinds of laborers have played varying roles in supporting or overthrowing the system, in seeking political alliances with each other or alternatively with surplus appropriators. In slavery, for example, field and house slaves exhibited varying relationships. So too did serfs assigned to agriculture versus crafts. Capitalism has had its blue and white collar employees. To Marx's credit, his surplus theory—and the class analysis built on it—grasped the deeper, systemic importance of these differences.

Capitalists distribute surpluses to yet other sorts of recipients for other purposes. For example, capitalists distribute surpluses as funds to managers charged with purchasing and installing more or better machines, tools, equipment, etc. Their goals might be to increase the scale of production or to replace labor power (automation) or both. What drives such distributions of the surplus is the competition among capitalists. Each fears that competitors will acquire machines or other inputs that enable more products at a lower cost; each hopes to be such an acquirer. With similar motivations, capitalists can direct surplus distributions to cover costs of relocating production to lower wage areas or recruiting workers from elsewhere (i.e., immigrants and outsourced labor) willing to work at lower wages.

Capitalists distribute portions of the surpluses they appropriate to fund whatever other conditions of existence that seem to them to need it.

For production sites threatened by thievery, for example, surplus may pay wages for the unproductive labor of security officers. Where productive laborers exhibit alcohol-related problems, capitalists may hire the unproductive labor power of personnel managers or counselors to help solve those problems. If litigation is a risk, capitalists will use surpluses to retain lawyers. Portions of the surplus must also be paid to federal, state, and/or local governments in taxes, dividends to shareholders, interest to lenders, and so on.

For Marx, the capitalist functions at the center of a complex system. On the one hand, the capitalist strives to appropriate the greatest possible surplus from hired productive laborers. On the other hand, the same capitalist must guess how best to distribute different portions of the appropriated surplus to various recipients (enablers, unproductive laborers) who provide conditions of existence for the capitalist enterprise.

No wonder capitalism develops unevenly—as Marx stressed. Each competing capitalist decides and functions around guesses about present and future realities. Each capitalist guesses differently because the circumstances of each and how these circumstances are assessed and understood vary. One succeeds and another fails giving capitalism its uneven development path. Deep suspicions of one another and even deeper suspicion of any state coordination keep capitalists from overcoming the systemic unevenness. Likewise, capitalism develops unevenly geographically as "developed" and "undeveloped" areas proliferate and even sometimes replace one another.

" Hegel remarks somewhere that all great world-historic facts and personages appear, so to speak, twice. He forgot to add: the first time as a tragedy, the second time as a farce. "

CHAPTER 6

How Contradictions Are Key in Marx's Analysis of Capitalism

Another remarkable quality of Marx's and many Marxists' analyses, besides specific insights drawn from their surplus-focused analysis, is their attention to contradictions. Beyond the tendencies they find shaping societies, they usually seek and find counteracting tendencies and likewise elements inside all tendencies that push them and society in different and often clashing directions. This sensitivity to and interest in contradictions derives in part from Marx's teacher, the German philosopher Hegel. In Hegel's view, everything is contradictory. Everything in life (nature, society, etc.) is a bundle of conflicting needs, forces, and pressures. Indeed, our thoughts about and knowledge of life are also inescapably contradictory.

For Marx, capitalism too exemplifies contradictions. As one example, Marx explains to us that every capitalist tries to get as much surplus from productive workers as possible. The more surplus that is appropriated, the more can be distributed as dividends to keep shareholders happy, as high salaries to motivate managers, etc. The surplus distributions keep the capitalist system going, reinforcing the capitalists' dominance. Since more surplus available to the capitalist is better, capitalists always seek more.

Greed is not the cause of capitalists' behavior; it is a quality they acquire in accommodating to and internalizing the requirements of competitive survival within the capitalist system.

Capitalists may appropriate more surplus if they reduce workers' wages while getting the same output from them. There are alternative ways to accomplish such wage reductions. Immigration of lower wage workers is a famous phenomenon in capitalist societies past and present. So too is switching from one population group to another (for example, from men to women, from adults to children, from one ethnicity to another, and so on). Of course, both these wage-reduction mechanisms entail contradictions as displaced wage-earners resent and resist. That may place new demands on capitalists' surpluses (say to offset enterprise damage from angry displaced workers) that nullify the gains from lower wages and so on. Lower-paid workers may display less loyalty to the enterprise. The contradictions abound and may, depending on the larger social context, overwhelm the initial capitalist impulse/tendency to lower wages.

Besides lowering wages, production costs may be reduced when capitalists can replace productive workers with machines. To automate, computerize, or robotize may be cheaper than—and therefore substitute for—hiring productive workers. However, no sooner do capitalists succeed in paying lower wages and/or hiring fewer workers, than they may well face another contradiction. The workers may now have less income than they had before because wages fell or automation hit. Thus they will be less able to buy what capitalists need to sell. To benefit by lowering their outlays to workers, capitalists have inadvertently undermined the demand for their products. The virtually universal drive to economize on labor costs operates in contradiction to the parallel drive to sell all that is produced.

The system is a contradiction: the very logic imposed on the capitalist undermines the overall success of the capitalist. For Marxists, no law, rule, regulation, or behavior pattern provides an escape from this contradiction; none ever has.

Capitalism experiences this contradiction in the form of recurring oscillations between periods of profit-boosting savings on labor costs and profit-busting insufficiencies of effective demand for capitalist products. That is how this system works. And of course, workers laid off because of automation or deficient demand may well worsen that deficiency and thereby produce a spiral downward into major recession or depression. Eventually, downturns produce a sufficient cheapening of labor power and produced inputs to enable capitalists to profit from resuming production. Then an upswing follows and repeats the same pattern of cyclical instability yet again.

Because of this and other contradictions explored across the three volumes of *Capital*, the capitalist system is profoundly unstable. Every four to seven years on average, wherever it has existed, capitalism produced an economic downturn. Workers suddenly lost jobs, businesses collapsed, and real mass suffering ensued for months or years. This instability occurred in addition to the destabilizing effects of natural disasters (floods, droughts, etc.) and of social disasters (wars). Any individual exhibiting a personal instability comparable to the economic and social instability of capitalism would long ago have been required to seek professional help and to make basic changes.

Marx's basic point is that capitalism produces and reproduces inequality and instability. That alone suggests we ought to challenge anyone who accepts a system that works this way.

Through the work of Marx and others, we can now recognize capitalism's contradictions plus the inadequacies and injustices they impose on us. It is precisely how the system works—how in particular it produces, appropriates, and distributes its surpluses—that proved to be the obstacle preventing capitalism from realizing liberty, equality, brotherhood, and democracy. And by focusing us on the organization of the surplus, Marx also provided us with the knowledge that the next system must be one in which the organization of the surplus is democratic, where those who produce the surplus are identical with those who appropriate it, and where the productive and unproductive laborers together and democratically decide who gets what portions of the surplus to perform what social services.

66 The philosophers have only interpreted the world, in various ways. The point, however, is to change it. 99

CHAPTER 7

What Marx Meant by Socialism Doing Better than Capitalism

I n the closing parts of this essay, we look at Marx's and Marxists' suggestions of solutions for the problems of capitalism's inadequacies. Marx himself said and wrote little about the future beyond capitalism. He didn't believe in future-gazing; no one could know how the world would evolve. Marx gave us some ideas of what might have to happen if we were going to get beyond capitalism. But he offered no blueprints or road maps. Later Marxists did not always share these hesitations, especially after Marxists came to play leading roles in what they called "socialist" societies.

Marx never suggested, contrary to what so many have said, that the state—the government—had to play some sort of ongoing, central role in what this future post-capitalist world would look like. Some later Marxists interpreted him to have suggested that, but it's hard to find within Marx's writings any idea like that. He never wrote a book about the state, because it wasn't the center or focus of his analyses. That focus was rather the relationships among people as they go about producing their existence: relationships such as master-slave, lord-serf, and employer-employee. In each one of those relationships, a minority of people makes all the key production decisions: masters, lords, employers. They decide what gets produced, how it gets produced, where it gets produced, and what is done with the surplus appropriated from productive workers.

To achieve a society that exhibits liberty, equality, fraternity, and democracy, the object to change first and foremost is production.

There has to be a fundamental change in how production gets done: at the office, factory, store, or home, wherever work gets done. For Marx, the goal of such change is to end the dichotomy between a few surplus-appropriators at the top of the workplace, those who make the key production-related decisions, and everybody else engaged at that workplace. No more mass of people producing or enabling a surplus that flows into the hands of a small surplus-appropriating minority. The goal is a different economic system, one in which the workplace becomes fundamentally egalitarian and democratic. The producers of the surplus become identically the appropriators and distributors of that surplus; exploitation thus ends. The decisions at the workplace—what, how, and where to produce and how to distribute the surplus—must be made democratically by productive and unproductive workers together on the basis of one-person, one-vote.

In this view, democratizing the workplace is how we conceptualize "doing better" than capitalism.

If you believe in democracy, if you believe that freedom for adults requires a democratic social environment, then that democracy must include your workplaces. That is where most adults spend most of their time, or at least major parts of it. Thus the solution for capitalism's problems requires transforming the capitalist workplace. What must go is the top-down, dichotomized hierarchy of employer at the top, mass of employees at the bottom. Instead, workplaces become democratic institutions where everyone has an equal say on what happens there. What must happen to the economy is like what many democrats have long advocated for politics. After all, ridding ourselves of kings, czars, and emperors proceeded on the grounds that subjection to a tiny group of people making all basic political decisions for all of us was unacceptable.

The same logic can apply to economics; indeed that is one way to grasp Marx's argument.

The democratization of politics has been a mantra, has been a slogan, and has been a goal for a long time.

Marx asks: why only the democratization of politics? Why not the democratization of the economy?

To go a step further, Marx effectively argues that a genuine political democracy requires an economic democracy as its ground and partner.

If we permit any economic system to enrich only a few, those rich will use their wealth to corrupt the political system so it secures their wealth. The histories of feudalism, slavery, and capitalism attest to this truth repeatedly. Today's gaudy spectacle of billionaires competing to buy votes is being lived by every reader of these lines.

One implication of Marx's gesturing towards a different, democratic way of organizing workplaces is that it will never suffice to go beyond capitalism if we merely replace private entrepreneurs or private employers with state officials. Nationalization or socialization of the means of production will not get us beyond capitalism in so far as it retains the employer versus employee dichotomy. Over the last hundred years, when state capitalism has replaced private capitalism, it has led some to refer to such state capitalism as socialism or even communism. Thus some people refer to state-run post offices, railway systems, or banks as evidence of socialism. Other people reserved the term socialism for whole societies that instituted state capitalism as their prevailing economic system such as the USSR, the People's Republic of China, and so on.

Of course, definitions can and do vary. The point of studying Marx is to be clear that in his analysis, replacing private capitalist exploiters with state officials in the parallel relationship with productive and unproductive workers is not the going beyond capitalism he had in mind in his critique of capitalism.

Capitalism is superseded when the workplace relationship designated by the term exploitation ends. That happens when productive laborers no longer deliver the surpluses they produce into the hands of others who appropriate and distribute them and make all the key decisions about those distributions.

Is the realization of Marx's solution merely a utopian dream? I don't think so. Indeed, I think many human beings have understood and supported Marx's way of thinking. That is why ideas of cooperative, communal, and other sorts of more democratic workplace organizations have been discussed and tried repeatedly across human history everywhere. Early American history had worker cooperatives: workers in farms, stores, small craft enterprises, getting together in democratic, egalitarian ways. Today, Spain has a famous example in the Mondragon Cooperative Corporation. Emilia Romagna in Italy is a place where roughly 40 percent of businesses are run as worker cooperatives, etc.

Marx's is a more formal and fuller statement of one version of these ideas. He worked it out a bit further into a modern formulation. Marx teaches it in a systematic, theoretically sophisticated way. Yet in doing so, he re-coups for us the history of many efforts over many years in virtually all cultures to move in that direction to achieve a just society.

Marx was a social critic for whom capitalism was not the end of human history. It was just the latest phase and badly needed the transition to something better.

Marx's work can remind us that capitalism's propo-nents and celebrants often make the same mistake as the proponents and celebrants of slavery and feudalism before them. They imagine wishfully that their system is the end of history, that their preferred system is as good as it can ever be, that humankind cannot do bet-ter. Every single one of those people has been proven wrong. Why then believe people who tell us today that we can't do better than capitalism? Marx, like many other historians, had noticed that economic systems such as feudalism, slavery, and all others had histories; they were born, evolved over time, died, and gave way to another system. By the 1850s, capitalism had shown Marx enough for him to seek its replacement by some-thing better. His analysis was the fruit of that seeking.

Americans especially now confront serious questions and evidence that our capitalist system is in trouble. It clearly serves the 1 percent far, far better than what it is doing to the vast mass of the people. For a while, mass bitterness, decline, and anger may be deflected away from the critique of a dysfunctional economic system.

For a while, this anger can be used to scapegoat immigrants, trade partners, minorities, and others among a sadly familiar set of candidates. But scapegoating has not solved problems. It does not do so today. Sooner or later, those serious about the problems and finding solutions will, as they always have, find their way to Marx and the Marxist tradition as a rich resource. To assist that process is the purpose of this essay.

" The proletarians have nothing to lose but their chains. They have a world to win. Working Men of All Countries, Unite! **"**

QUOTES BY KARL MARX

Why Understanding Capitalism Today Requires Marxism

"The history of all hitherto existing society is the history of class struggles." Marx, K., & Engels, F. (1966). *Manifesto of the Communist Party.* Moscow: Progress Publishers.

Capitalism vs. Slavery and Feudalism: Achievements and Failures

"The mode of production of materials life determines the social, political and intellectual life process in general." Marx, K. (1970). *A Contribution to the Critique of Political Economy.* Moscow: Progress Publishers.

Employer/Employee: The Core Relationship of Capitalism

"The human being is in the most literal sense a political animal, not merely a gregarious animal, but an animal which can individuate itself only in the midst of society." Marx, K., & Nicolaus, M. (1973). *Grundrisse: Foundations of the Critique of Political Economy.* New York: Vintage Books.

Employers/Employees: Capitalism's Struggling Classes

"As in private life one differentiates between what a man thinks and says of himself and what he really is and does, so in historical struggles one must still more distinguish the language and the imaginary aspirations of parties from their real organism and their real interests, their conception of themselves from their reality." Marx, K., & De, L. D. (1898). *The Eighteenth Brumaire of Louis Bonaparte*. New York: International Pub. Co.

Producing and Distributing the Surplus in the Capitalist System

"As capitalist, he is only capital personified. His soul is the soul of capital. But capital has one single life impulse, the tendency to create value and surplus-value, to make its constant factor, the means of production, absorb the greatest possible amount of surplus-labour." Marx, Karl, 1818-1883. (1959). *Das Kapital: A Critique of Political Economy*. Chicago: H. Regnery.

How Contradictions Are Key in Marx's Analysis of Capitalism

"Hegel remarks somewhere that all great world-historic facts and personages appear, so to speak, twice. He forgot to add: the first time as a tragedy, the second time as a farce." Marx, K., & De, L. D. (1898). *The Eighteenth Brumaire of Louis Bonaparte*. New York: International Pub. Co.

What Marx Meant by Socialism Doing Better than Capitalism

"The philosophers have only interpreted the world, in various ways. The point, however, is to change it." Karl Marx, "Theses on Feuerbach," in Marx, K. (1975). *Karl Marx and Fredrick Engels: Selected Works.* Moscow: Progress Publishers.

Quotes

"The proletarians have nothing to lose but their chains. They have a world to win. Working Men of All Countries, Unite!" Marx, K., & Engels, F. (1966). *Manifesto of the Communist Party.* Moscow: Progress Publishers.

ACKNOWLEDGMENTS

The dynamic center of capitalism is abandoning the United States and, more broadly, the G7. It is relocating to China and the BRICS. That relocation is affecting capitalism everywhere. Like every empire before, the American empire that dominated the world economy over the century ending in 2015 is now in its period of decline. To understand what this means for the future of capitalism and socialism in both areas, it is more important than ever to preserve, transmit, and further develop and extend the Marxian critical tradition. By its focus on capitalism as a system and on transition to an economic system better than capitalism, Marxism offers and enables unique insights and thus means of advance. Capitalist societies have mostly repressed or ignored Marxism because of its persuasive power and social effects. Among my many colleagues, students, and fellow activists—and especially in and around the growing www.DemocracyatWork.info community—many have contributed to producing this book. I want to thank them for thereby contributing to the further growth and spread of the Marxist tradition of critical social thought and action aimed at doing better than capitalism.

FURTHER READING

David M. Brennan, David Kristjanson-Gural, Catherine P. Mulder and Eruk. K. Olsen, editors, *Routledge Handbook of Marxian Economic*, Routledge, 2017.

Theodore Burczak, Robert Garnett, and Richard McIntyre, editors, *Knowledge, Class and Economics: Marxism Without Guarantees*, Routledge, 2018.

Stephen Resnick and Richard Wolff. *Knowledge and Class: A Marxian Critique of Political Economy*, University of Chicago Press, 1987.

Stephen Resnick and Richard Wolff, *Class Theory and History: Capitalism and Communism in the USSR*, Routledge Publishers, 2002.

Stephen Resnick and Richard Wolff, editors, *New Departures in Marxian Theory*, Routledge, 2006.

Richard D. Wolff and Stephen A. Resnick, *Contending Economic Theories: Neoclassical, Keynesian and Marxian*, MIT Press, 2012.

Richard D. Wolff, *Democracy at Work: A Cure for Capitalism*, Haymarket Books, 2016.

Richard D. Wolff, *Understanding Marxism*, Haymarket Books, 2025.

Richard D. Wolff, *Understanding Socialism*, Haymarket Books, 2025.

INDEX

employers distributing
surpluses to self and
employees, 12–13
employers' efforts to
increase size of
surplus, 28, 31
goal to achieve fairer
distribution of, 44–45
Marx on surplus labor,
11–12, 17–25
Marx's unique concept of
class based on, 23–25
minority appropriating
surpluses produced by
majority, 22–23
need for democratic
process for
organization of, 41

Thomas Aquinas, Saint, xii

unproductive laborers, 19,
20, 41
USSR (Soviet Union), xiii–
xiv, xix, 32–34, 46

value added, 21

wage-reduction,
contradictions in, 38
"wage slave," Marx on, 23
Wolff, Richard, personal
background of,
xvi–xviii

worker cooperatives, xv, xxi,
xxii, 47
workplace, 45, 46, 47
employer/employee
struggles, ix–x
employer's controlling,
13, 44

Yale University, xvi–xvii

Zola, Émile, 8

ABOUT THE AUTHOR

Richard D. Wolff is professor of economics emeritus, University of Massachusetts, Amherst, and a visiting professor at the New School University in New York. Together with the organization he helped to found, Democracy at Work, Wolff produces the weekly program *Economic Update* (which he also hosts). That program is syndicated on 100 radio stations nationwide as well as broadcast on YouTube where Democracy at Work has over 500,000 subscribers. He is the author of numerous books, including *Democracy at Work* and, most recently, *The Sickness Is the System*.

ABOUT HAYMARKET BOOKS

Haymarket Books is a radical, independent, nonprofit book publisher based in Chicago. Our mission is to publish books that contribute to struggles for social and economic justice. We strive to make our books a vibrant and organic part of social movements and the education and development of a critical, engaged, and internationalist left.

We take inspiration and courage from our namesakes, the Haymarket Martyrs, who gave their lives fighting for a better world. Their 1886 struggle for the eight-hour day—which gave us May Day, the international workers' holiday—reminds workers around the world that ordinary people can organize and struggle for their own liberation. These struggles—against oppression, exploitation, environmental devastation, and war—continue today across the globe.

Since our founding in 2001, Haymarket has published more than nine hundred titles. Radically independent, we seek to drive a wedge into the risk-averse world of corporate book publishing. Our authors include Angela

Y. Davis, Arundhati Roy, Keeanga-Yamahtta Taylor, Eve Ewing, Aja Monet, Mariame Kaba, Naomi Klein, Rebecca Solnit, Olúfẹ́mi O. Táíwò, Mohammed El-Kurd, José Olivarez, Noam Chomsky, Winona LaDuke, Robyn Maynard, Leanne Betasamosake Simpson, Howard Zinn, Mike Davis, Marc Lamont Hill, Dave Zirin, Astra Taylor, and Amy Goodman, among many other leading writers of our time. We are also the trade publishers of the acclaimed Historical Materialism Book Series.

Haymarket also manages a vibrant community organizing and event space in Chicago, Haymarket House, the popular Haymarket Books Live event series and podcast, and the annual Socialism Conference.